Contents

TITLE	PAGE NUMBERS			
	C Treble Instruments	B♭ Instruments	E♭ Instruments	C Bass Clef Instruments
Away in a Manger	4	15	26	37
The First Noël	5	16	27	38
Go, Tell It on the Mountain	6	17	28	39
Hark! The Herald Angels Sing	7	18	29	40
Jingle Bells	8	19	30	41
Joy to the World	9	20	31	42
O Come, All Ye Faithful (Adeste Fideles)	10	21	32	43
O Holy Night	12	22	34	44
Up on the Housetop	11	24	33	46
We Wish You a Merry Christmas	14	25	36	47

The Real Book Multi-Tracks Vol. 10

For C, B♭, E♭ & Bass Clef Instruments

CHRISTMAS SONGS

Play-Along

Recorded by Ric Probst at Tanner Monagle Studio
Trumpet: Jamie Breiwick
Alto and Tenor Sax: Eric Schoor
Piano: Mark Davis
Bass: Jeff Hamann
Drums: David Bayles

To access online content, visit:
www.halleonard.com/mylibrary

Enter Code
7163-3148-4339-2921

ISBN 978-1-4950-9702-7

7777 W. BLUEMOUND RD. P.O. BOX 13819 MILWAUKEE, WI 53213

In Australia Contact:
Hal Leonard Australia Pty. Ltd.
4 Lentara Court
Cheltenham, Victoria, 3192 Australia
Email: ausadmin@halleonard.com.au

For more information on the Real Book series, including community forums, please visit
www.OfficialRealBook.com

Visit Hal Leonard Online at
www.halleonard.com

THE FIRST NOËL

- W. SANDYS' CHRISTMAS CAROLS/
17ᵗʰ CENTURY ENGLISH CAROL

C VERSION

AFTER SOLOS, D.S. AL ⊕
(PLAY PICKUPS)

6

GO, TELL IT ON THE MOUNTAIN

(MED. FAST)
C VERSION

- AFRICAN-AMERICAN SPIRITUAL/
JOHN W. WORK, JR.

REPEAT HEAD IN
AFTER SOLOS, D.C. AL ⊕
HEAD OUT: TAKE ⊕ 3rd X

HARK! THE HERALD ANGELS SING

- Charles Wesley/George Whitefield/
Felix Mendelssohn-Bartholdy/William H. Cummings

(MED. FAST)

C VERSION

AFTER SOLOS,
D.C. AL ⊕

Jingle Bells

- J. Pierpont

Joy to the World

- Isaac Watts/Lowell Mason/George Frideric Handel

AFTER SOLOS,
D.C. AL ⊕

O HOLY NIGHT

- ADOLPHE ADAM

C VERSION

WE WISH YOU A MERRY CHRISTMAS

(FAST)

- TRADITIONAL ENGLISH FOLKSONG

C VERSION

REPEAT HEAD IN/OUT
AFTER SOLOS, D.S. AL ⊕
(PLAY PICKUP)

Away in a Manger

— James R. Murray/John T. McFarland

REPEAT HEAD IN/OUT
AFTER SOLOS, D.S. AL ⊕
(PLAY PICKUP)

THE FIRST NOËL

– W. SANDYS' CHRISTMAS CAROLS/
17th CENTURY ENGLISH CAROL

(MED.)

Bb VERSION

AFTER SOLOS, D.S. AL ⊕
(PLAY PICKUPS)

Go, Tell It On The Mountain

(MED. FAST)

B♭ Version

- African-American Spiritual/
John W. Work, Jr.

REPEAT HEAD IN
AFTER SOLOS, D.C. AL ⊕
HEAD OUT: TAKE ⊕ 3rd X

JOY TO THE WORLD

- Isaac Watts/Lowell Mason/George Frideric Handel

(MED. FAST)

Bb VERSION

AFTER SOLOS,
D.C. AL ⊕

O COME, ALL YE FAITHFUL
(ADESTE FIDELES)

- JOHN FRANCIS WADE

Bb VERSION

AFTER SOLOS, D.S. AL ⊕
(PLAY PICKUP)

O HOLY NIGHT

(Fast)

Bb VERSION

– ADOLPHE ADAM

AFTER SOLOS, D.C. AL ⊕

UP ON THE HOUSETOP

- B.R. HANBY

(FAST)

B♭ VERSION

REPEAT HEAD IN/OUT
AFTER SOLOS, D.C. AL ⊕

WE WISH YOU A MERRY CHRISTMAS

(Fast)

-- TRADITIONAL ENGLISH FOLKSONG

Bb VERSION

REPEAT HEAD IN/OUT
AFTER SOLOS, D.S. AL ⊕
(PLAY PICKUP)

Away in a Manger

- James R. Murray/John T. McFarland

Eᵇ Version

REPEAT HEAD IN/OUT
AFTER SOLOS, D.S. AL ⊕
(PLAY PICKUP)

THE FIRST NOËL

W. SANDYS' CHRISTMAS CAROLS/
17th CENTURY ENGLISH CAROL

Eb VERSION

(MED.)

AFTER SOLOS, D.S. AL ⊕
(PLAY PICKUPS)

GO, TELL IT ON THE MOUNTAIN

(MED. FAST)
Eb VERSION

- AFRICAN-AMERICAN SPIRITUAL/
JOHN W. WORK, JR.

REPEAT HEAD IN
AFTER SOLOS, D.C. AL ⊕
HEAD OUT: TAKE ⊕ 3rd X

HARK! THE HERALD ANGELS SING

- Charles Wesley/George Whitefield/
Felix Mendelssohn-Bartholdy/William H. Cummings

AFTER SOLOS,
D.C. AL ⊕

Jingle Bells

- J. Pierpont

(MED. FAST)

Eb VERSION

AFTER SOLOS, D.C. AL ⊕

JOY TO THE WORLD

- Isaac Watts/Lowell Mason/George Frideric Handel

O COME, ALL YE FAITHFUL
(ADESTE FIDELES)

- JOHN FRANCIS WADE

Eb VERSION

AFTER SOLOS, D.S. AL ⊕
(PLAY PICKUP)

UP ON THE HOUSETOP

- B.R. HANBY

(FAST)

Eb VERSION

REPEAT HEAD IN/OUT
AFTER SOLOS, D.C. AL ⊕

O HOLY NIGHT

— ADOLPHE ADAM

(FAST)

E♭ VERSION

WE WISH YOU A MERRY CHRISTMAS

(FAST)

Eb VERSION

— TRADITIONAL ENGLISH FOLKSONG

REPEAT HEAD IN/OUT
AFTER SOLOS, D.S. AL ⊕
(PLAY PICKUP)

Away In A Manger

- James R. Murray/John T. McFarland

BASS VERSION

(MED. SLOW)

REPEAT HEAD IN/OUT
AFTER SOLOS, D.S. AL ⊕
(PLAY PICKUP)

THE FIRST NOËL

- W. SANDYS' CHRISTMAS CAROLS/
17th CENTURY ENGLISH CAROL

(MED.)

BASS VERSION

AFTER SOLOS, D.S. AL ⊕
(PLAY PICKUPS)

Go, Tell It On The Mountain

– African-American Spiritual/
John W. Work, Jr.

(MED. FAST)
BASS VERSION

REPEAT HEAD IN
AFTER SOLOS, D.C. AL ⊕
HEAD OUT: TAKE ⊕ 3rd X

HARK! THE HERALD ANGELS SING

- CHARLES WESLEY/GEORGE WHITEFIELD/
FELIX MENDELSSOHN-BARTHOLDY/WILLIAM H. CUMMINGS

(MED. FAST)

BASS VERSION

AFTER SOLOS,
D.C. AL ⊕

Jingle Bells

- J. PIERPONT

Joy to the World

— Isaac Watts/Lowell Mason/George Frideric Handel

BASS VERSION

O COME, ALL YE FAITHFUL
(ADESTE FIDELES)

- JOHN FRANCIS WADE

AFTER SOLOS, D.S. AL ⊕
(PLAY PICKUP)

UP ON THE HOUSETOP

- B.R. HANBY

REPEAT HEAD IN/OUT
AFTER SOLOS, D.C. AL ⊕

WE WISH YOU A MERRY CHRISTMAS

(FAST)

- TRADITIONAL ENGLISH FOLKSONG

BASS VERSION

REPEAT HEAD IN/OUT
AFTER SOLOS, D.S. AL ⊕
(PLAY PICKUP)

THE REAL BOOK MULTI-TRACKS

1. MAIDEN VOYAGE PLAY-ALONG

Autumn Leaves • Blue Bossa • Doxy • Footprints • Maiden Voyage • Now's the Time • On Green Dolphin Street • Satin Doll • Summertime • Tune Up.
00196616 Book with Online Media $17.99

2. MILES DAVIS PLAY-ALONG

Blue in Green • Boplicity (Be Bop Lives) • Four • Freddie Freeloader • Milestones • Nardis • Seven Steps to Heaven • So What • Solar • Walkin'.
00196798 Book with Online Media $17.99

3. ALL BLUES PLAY-ALONG

All Blues • Back at the Chicken Shack • Billie's Bounce (Bill's Bounce) • Birk's Works • Blues by Five • C-Jam Blues • Mr. P.C. • One for Daddy-O • Reunion Blues • Turnaround.
00196692 Book with Online Media $17.99

4. CHARLIE PARKER PLAY-ALONG

Anthropology • Blues for Alice • Confirmation • Donna Lee • K.C. Blues • Moose the Mooche • My Little Suede Shoes • Ornithology • Scrapple from the Apple • Yardbird Suite.
00196799 Book with Online Media $17.99

5. JAZZ FUNK PLAY-ALONG

Alligator Bogaloo • The Chicken • Cissy Strut • Cold Duck Time • Comin' Home Baby • Mercy, Mercy, Mercy • Put It Where You Want It • Sidewinder • Tom Cat • Watermelon Man.
00196728 Book with Online Media $17.99

9. CHRISTMAS CLASSICS

Blue Christmas • Christmas Time Is Here • Frosty the Snow Man • Have Yourself a Merry Little Christmas • I'll Be Home for Christmas • My Favorite Things • Santa Claus Is Comin' to Town • Silver Bells • White Christmas • Winter Wonderland.
00236808 Book with Online Media $17.99

10. CHRISTMAS SONGS

Away in a Manger • The First Noel • Go, Tell It on the Mountain • Hark! the Herald Angels Sing • Jingle Bells • Joy to the World • O Come, All Ye Faithful • O Holy Night • Up on the Housetop • We Wish You a Merry Christmas.
00236809 Book with Online Media $17.99

The interactive, online audio interface includes:
• tempo control
• looping
• buttons to turn each instrument on or off
• lead sheet with follow-along marker
• melody performed by a saxophone or trumpet on the "head in" and "head out."

The full stereo tracks can also be downloaded and played off-line. Separate lead sheets are included for C, B-flat, E-flat and Bass Clef instruments.

HAL•LEONARD®
www.halleonard.com

Prices, content and availability subject to change without notice.